I Am The Door

By Natasha Guruleva

To Fred

© Natasha Guruleva. All Rights Reserved
No part of this book may be reproduced, stored in a retrieval system, or transmitted in any form, or by any means, electronic, mechanical, photocopying, recording, or otherwise, without prior permission of the copyright owner.
Photography: Alexander Krivenyshev, Gennady Smirnov, Natasha Guruleva
Text: Natasha Guruleva
Cover and interior page design by Natasha Guruleva

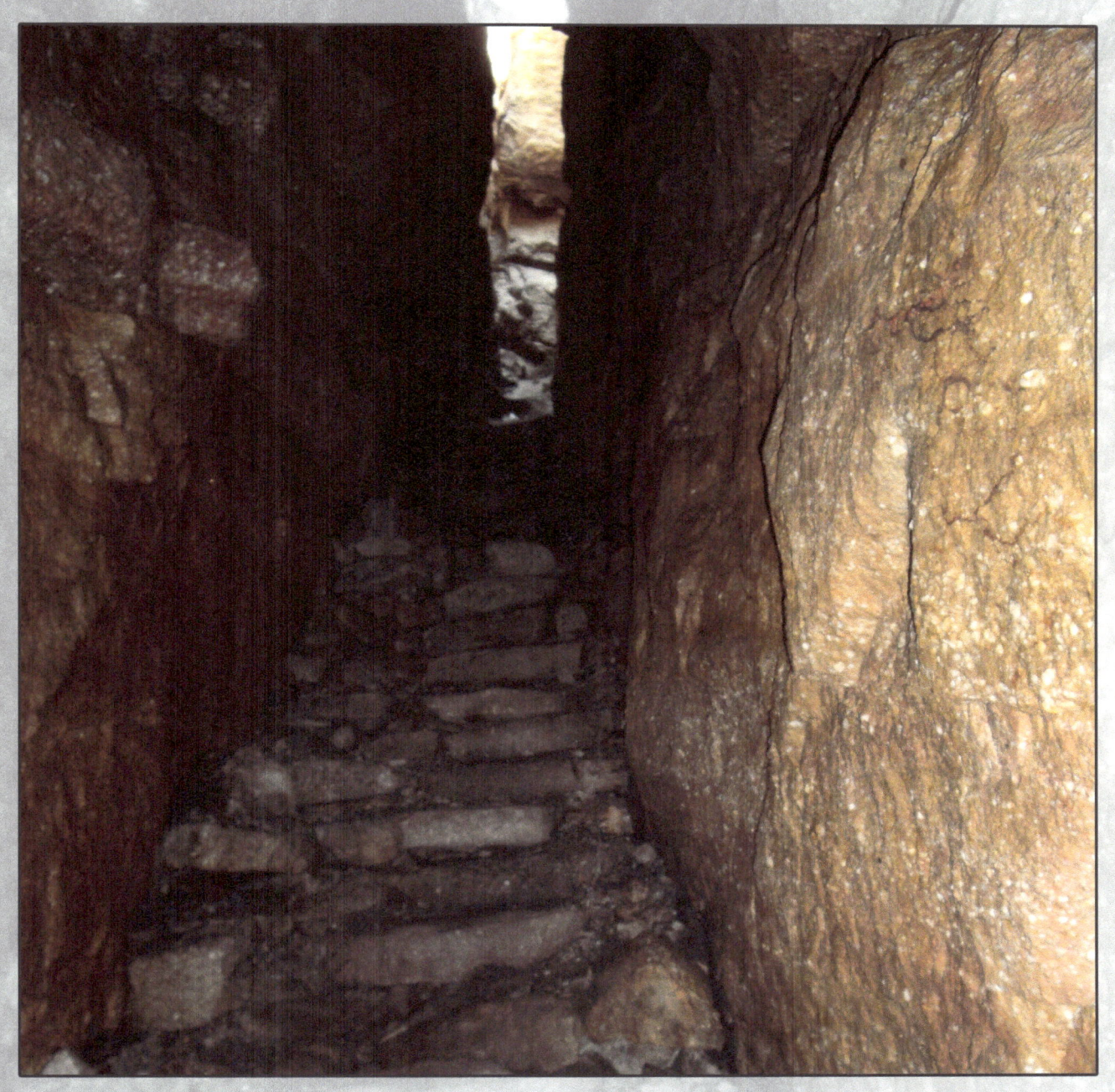

I am the door –

Between real and ethereal

Between solid and aerial

Between mundane and surreal

Between what is and what isn't

Many perish

Looking for me

     - I'm here and I'm not

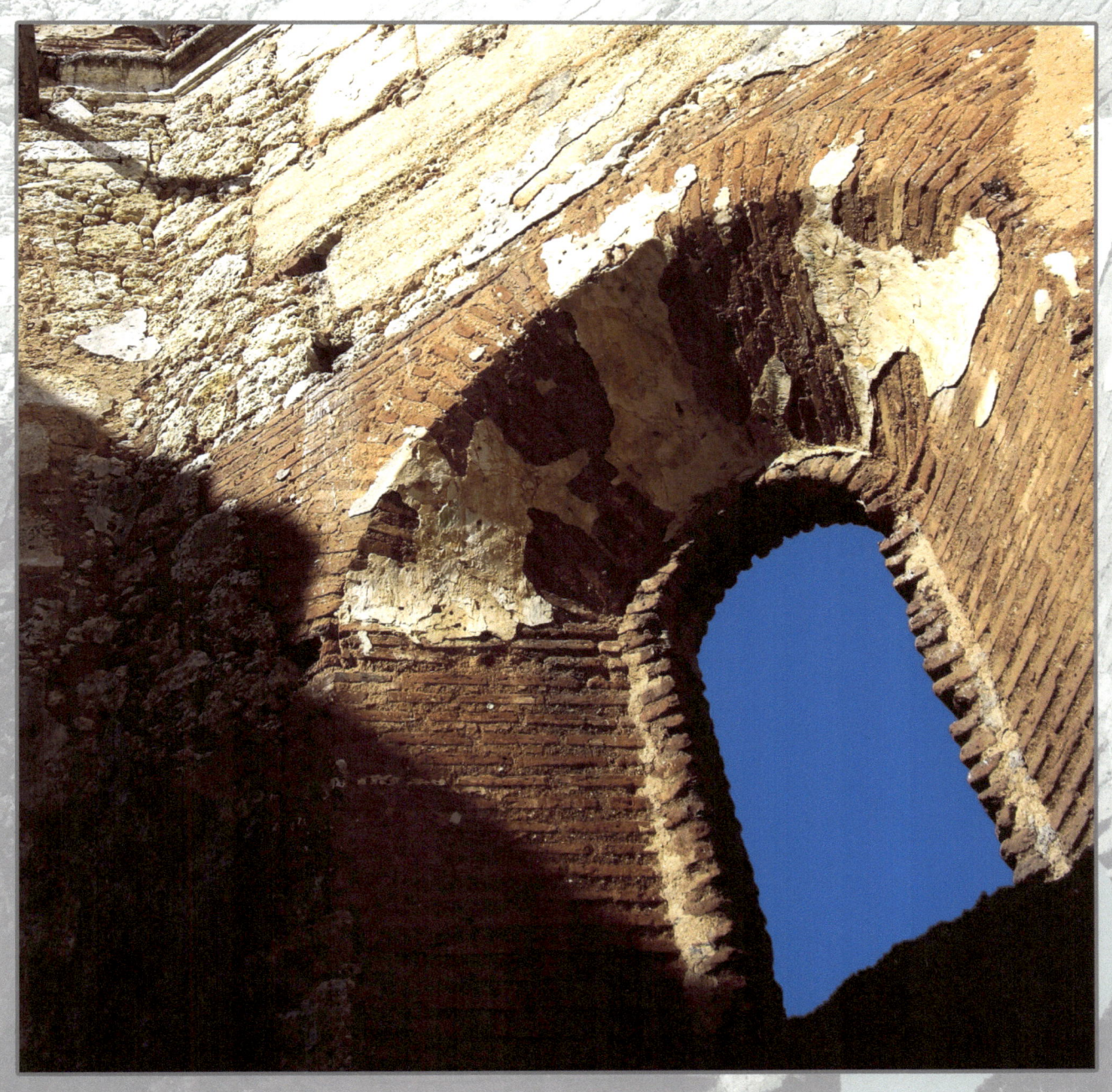

I am the door,

I am the gate.

Dispassionately

I look at everyone

Who attempts to enter.

I don't judge,

I don't have desires,

Aspirations, thoughts,

I am just there.

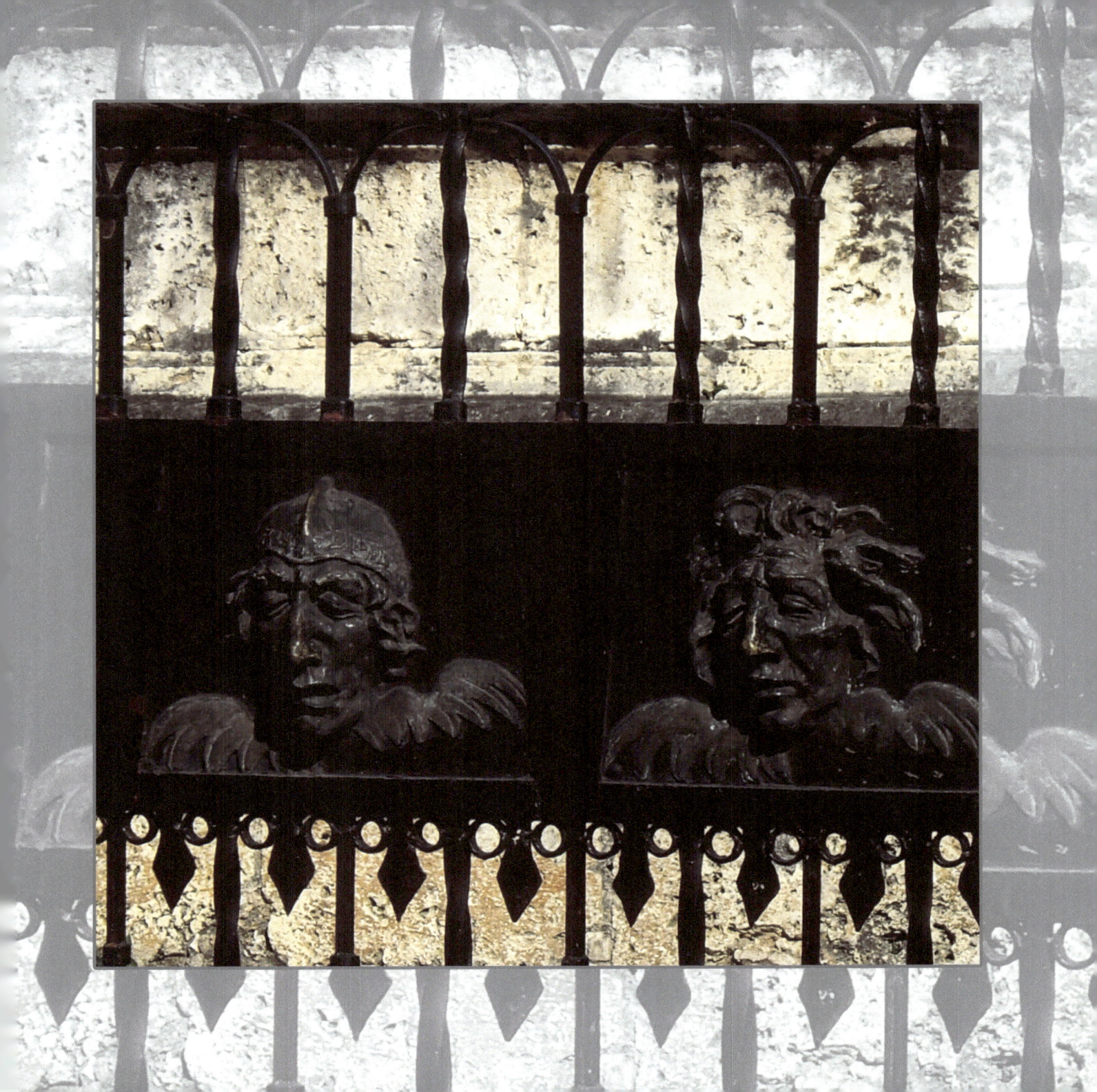

I am the door –

I guard the treasure.

See the line?

Stand at the end of it

      and wait.

I am the door.

Every day

The line grows longer and longer,

But I can't let them in –

Not without an "open-sesame."

They don't know it's that simple,

And I can't tell them –

Because I am just the door.

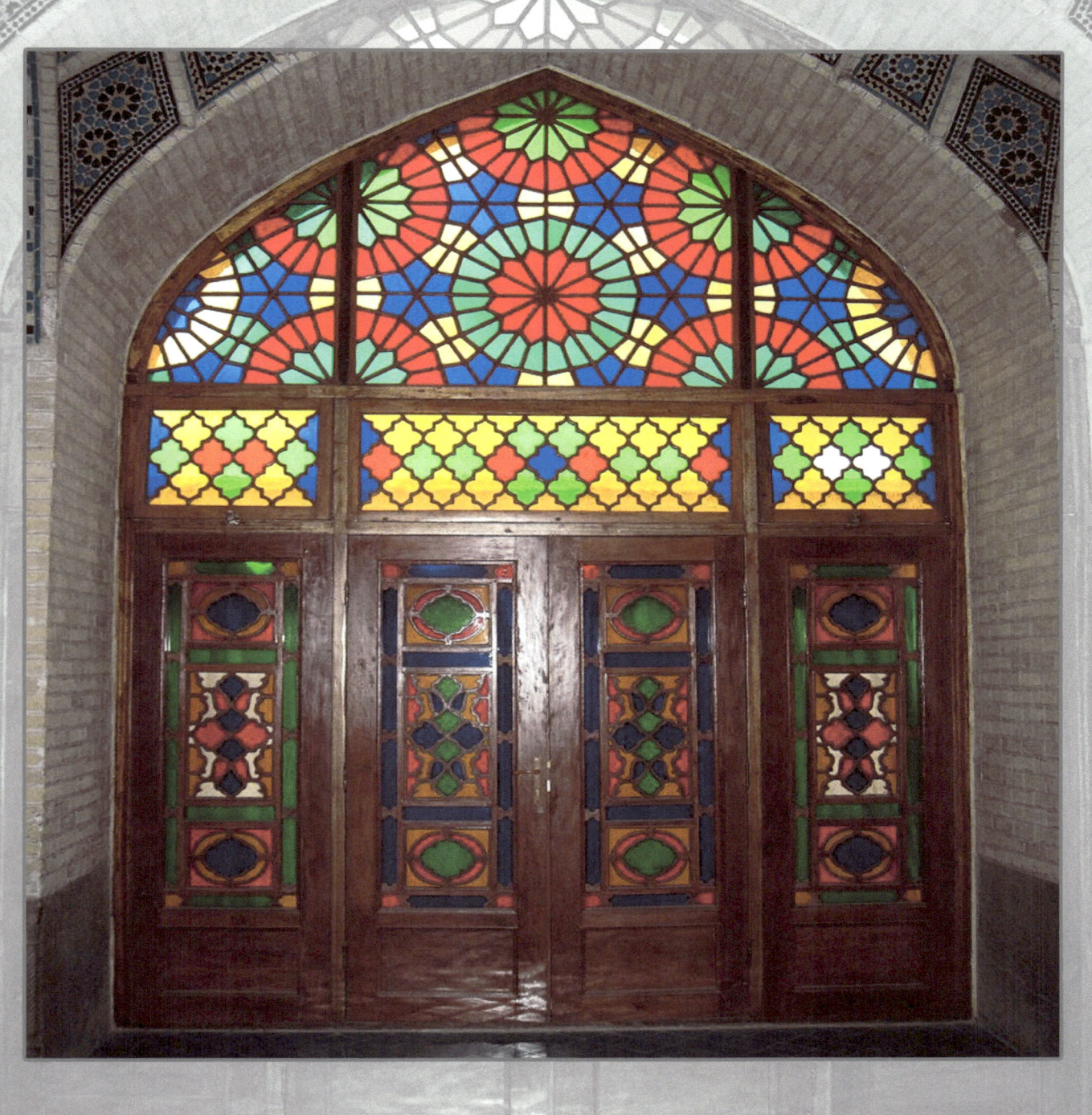

I am the door,

Through which

Everything comes

And goes away:

Your friends,

Your attachments,

Your possessions,

Your loves,

Your achievements,

Your memories –

Both good and bad.

I don't discriminate

Welcoming all

That passes through,

I don't feel sorry

For anything

That left you

While seeing it all –

Because I am the door.

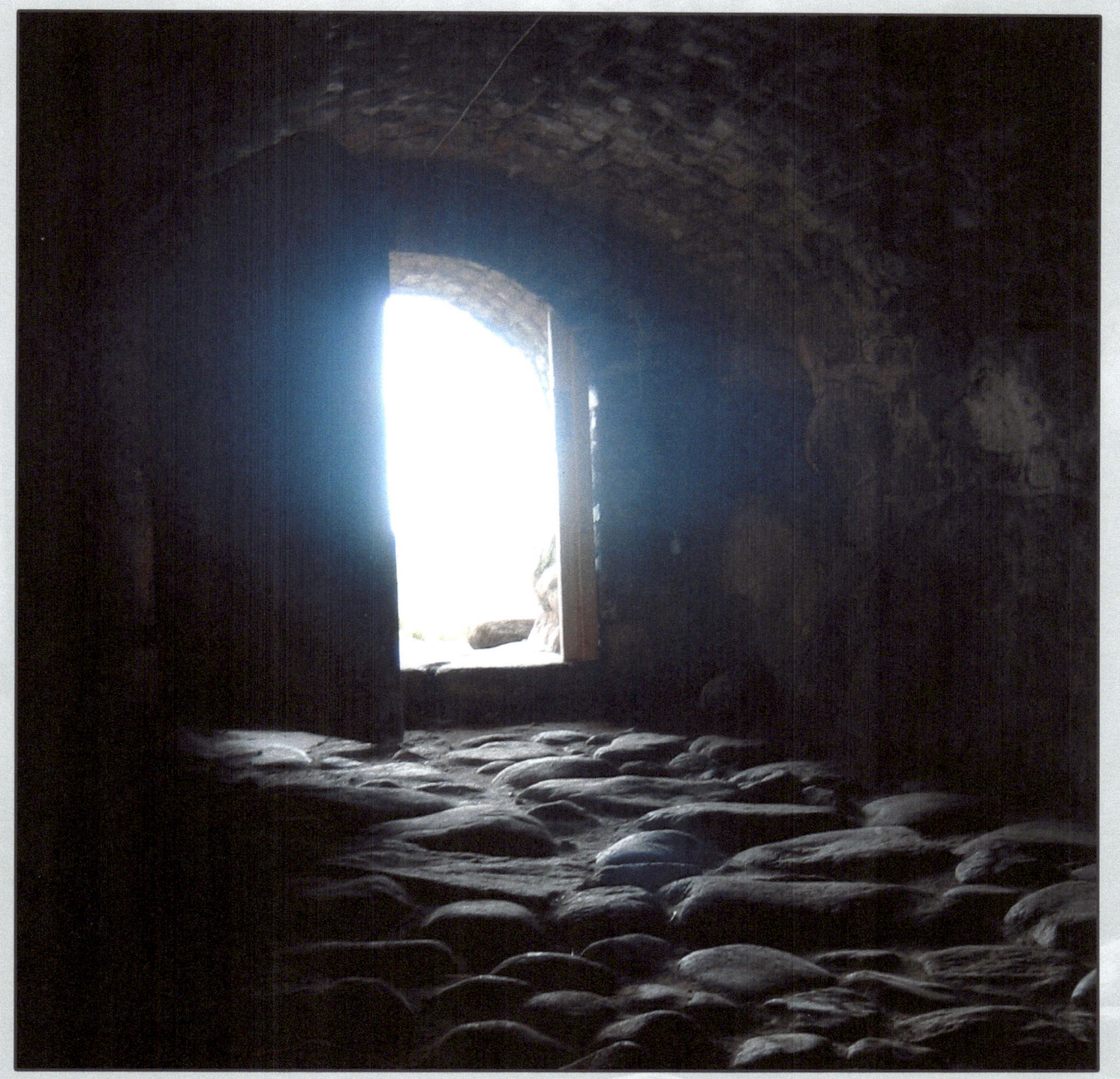

I am the door

Between life and death.

I am patient –

You have all the time in the world

To get ready,

You have time

To say goodbye,

To close your eyes,

To wave faraway.

You have eternity

To say hello to,

To open your eyes

The best you can,

To breathe

      Release.

I wouldn't push you,

I'll wait –

Cause I am the door.

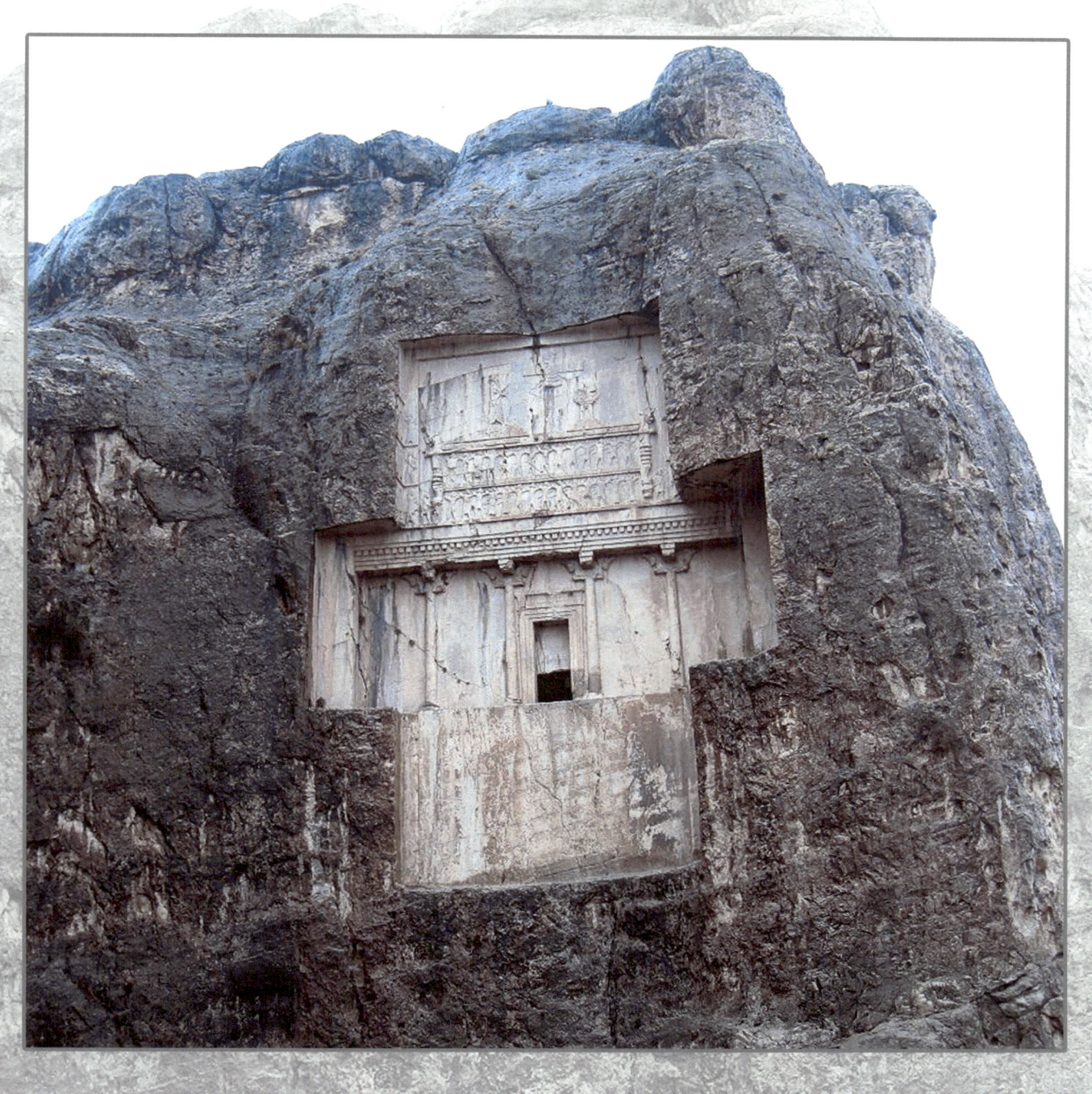

I am the door,
I am the way in
      And the way out,
I am sentence
      And hope,
I am death
      And life,
I am rise
      And fall,
I am a witness.

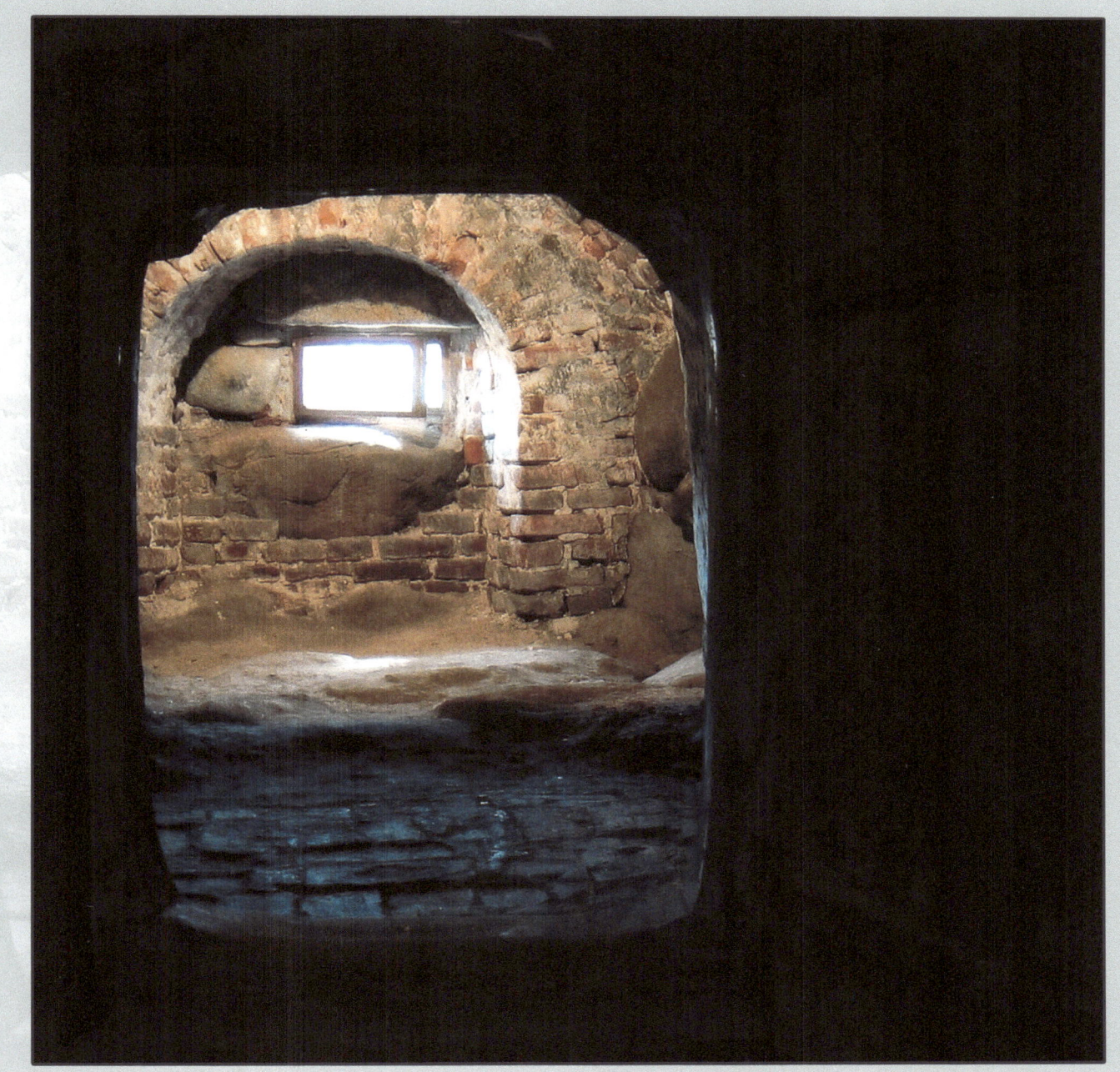

I am the door

Between good and evil.

They, who seek good,

Have to pass through me.

The ones who choose evil

Pass through me too.

I am the choice.

I can't show

Which side is good

And which side is bad –

Only let them through.

I am neither good nor bad –

Because I am just the door.

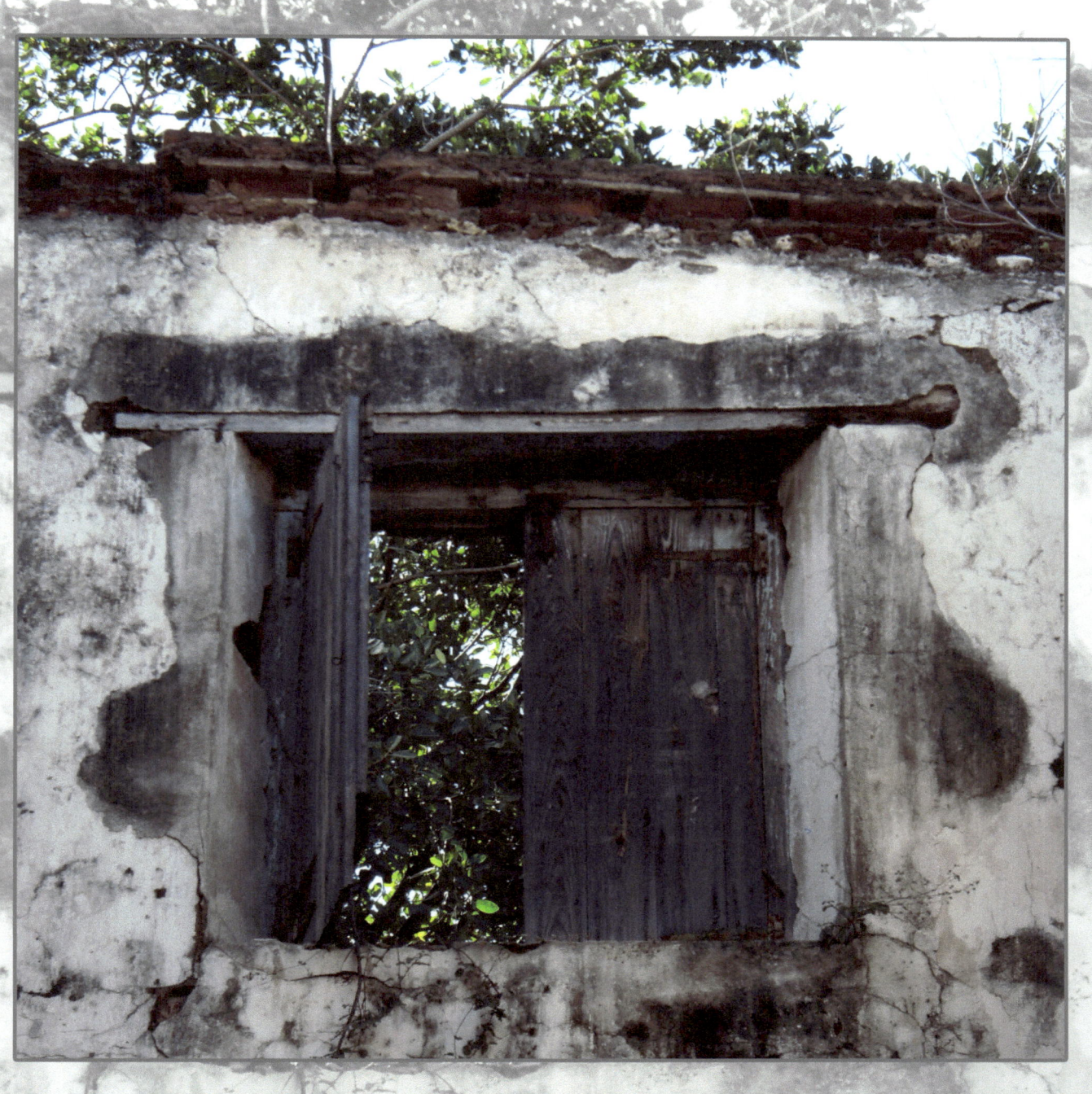

I am the door,

I am the gatekeeper.

I guard the way to the light

    Though I don't stop anyone

        who seeks it.

I watch the path

    to the darkness

        Though I don't warn anyone

        who falls in.

I belong to both.

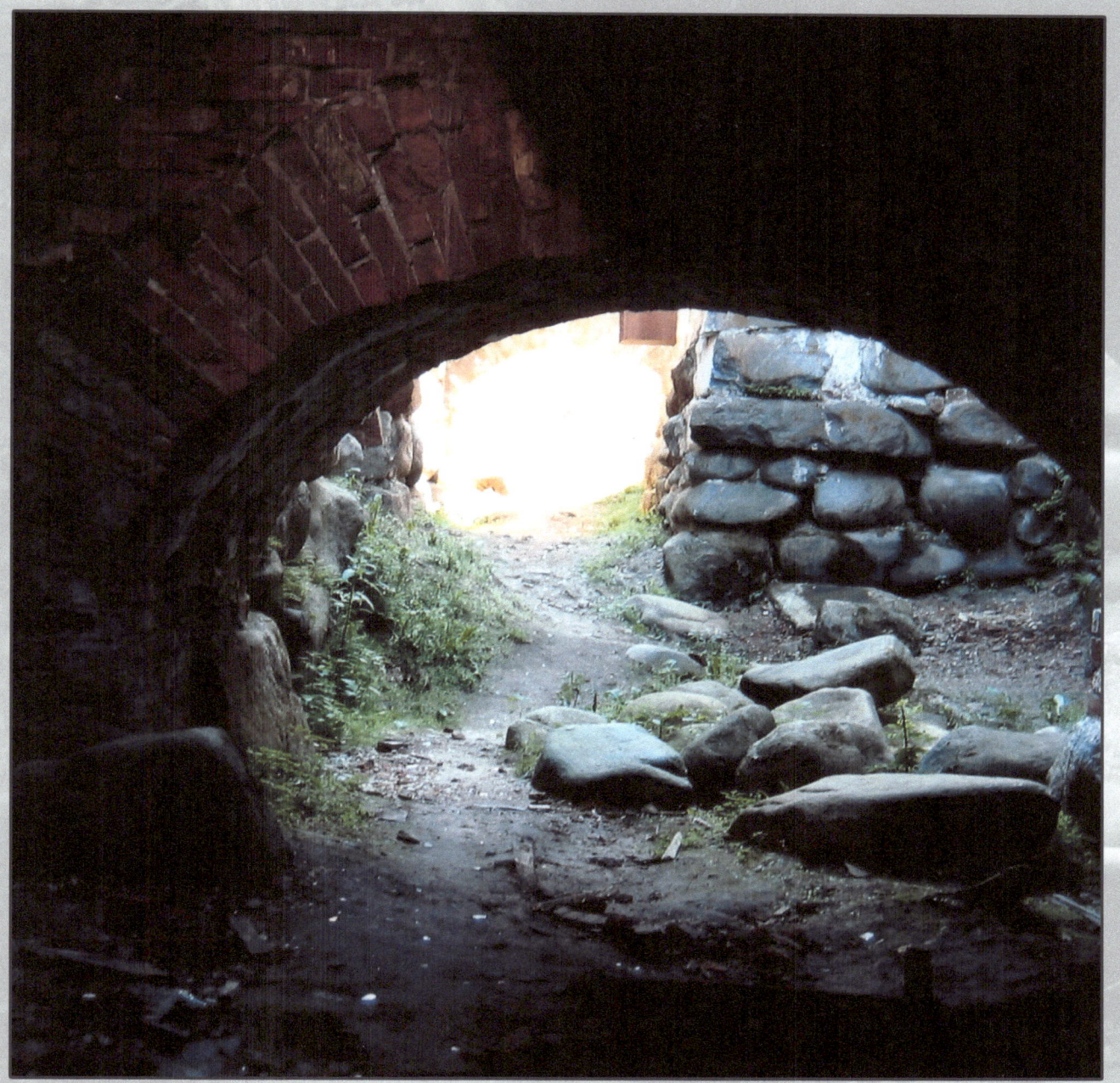

I am the door

That divides

The secular world

    and the Garden.

I can see it,

I can smell it,

I'm rapt in ecstasy

Of the others

Who crossed the threshold,

But I can never join them,

Can never share their delight

In walking the paths of the Garden,

Can never explode

  in laughter of joy

    of simply being there –

Because I am the door

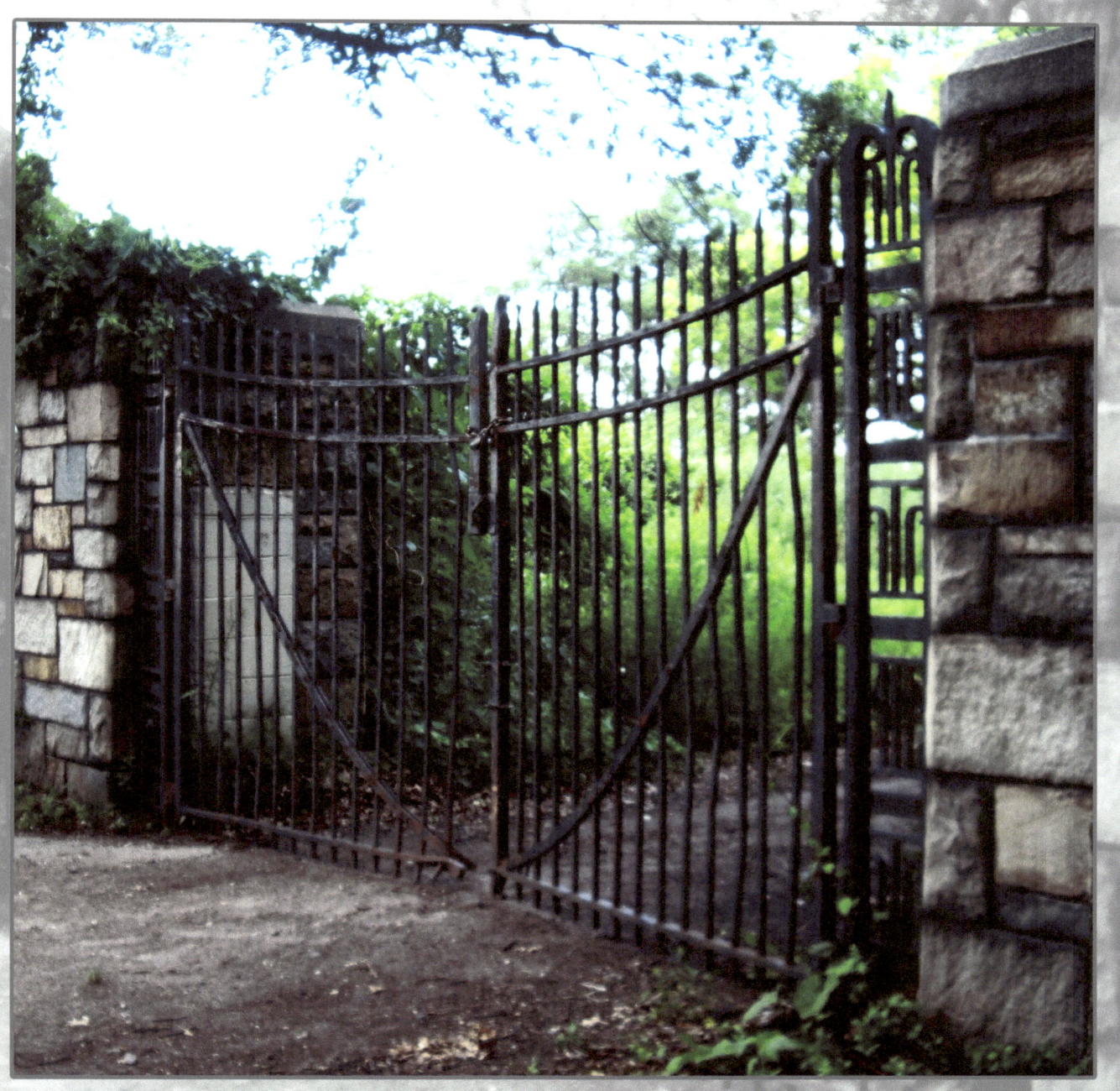

I am the door,
I am an object
    blocking your way,
I am a function
    implying your cooperation,
I am a meaning
    of your actions,
I am equal
    to your aspirations,
I am ajar.

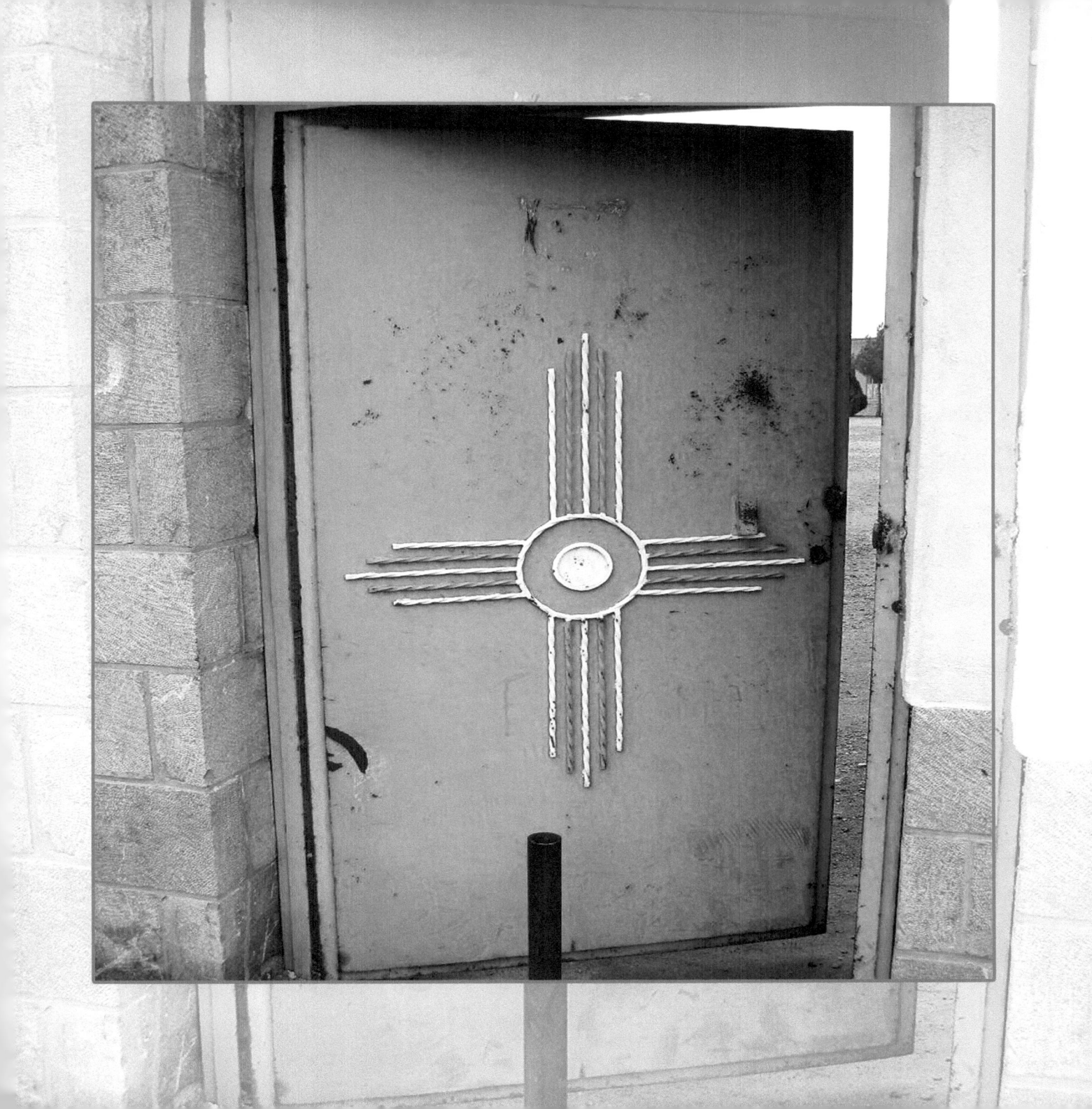

I am the door,

I am the earth's heart valve,

I conduct the orchestra

Of the ocean

      Holding the rhythm

For the waves

      To splash over the shore,

For the clouds

      To lisp their rise,

For the seagulls

      To voice their lines,

For the pebbles

To lead the percussions.

I am the door

Of the life's concert-hall.

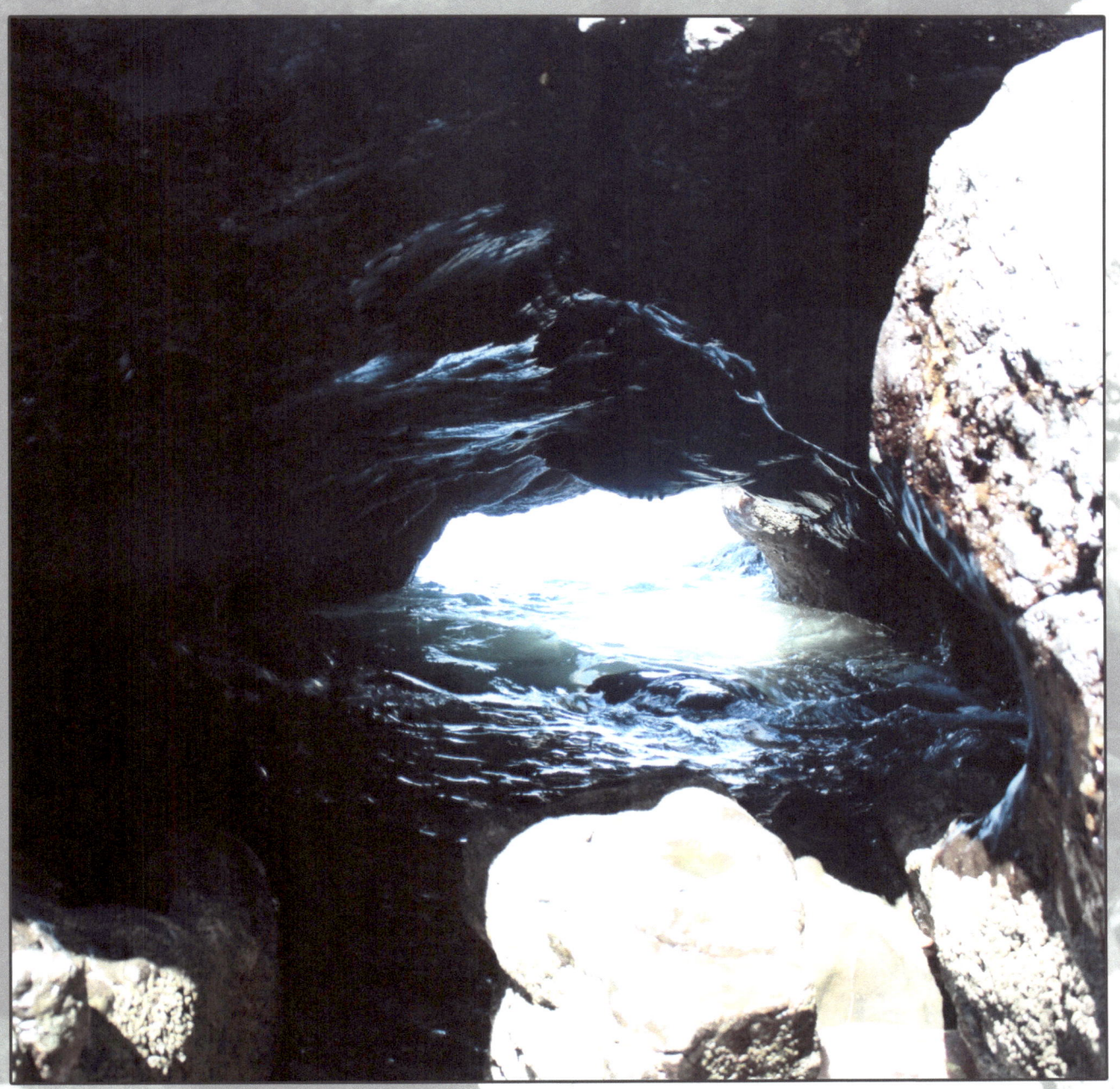

I am the door

I am the beginning

    And the end,

The entrance

    And the exit.

Where are you going?

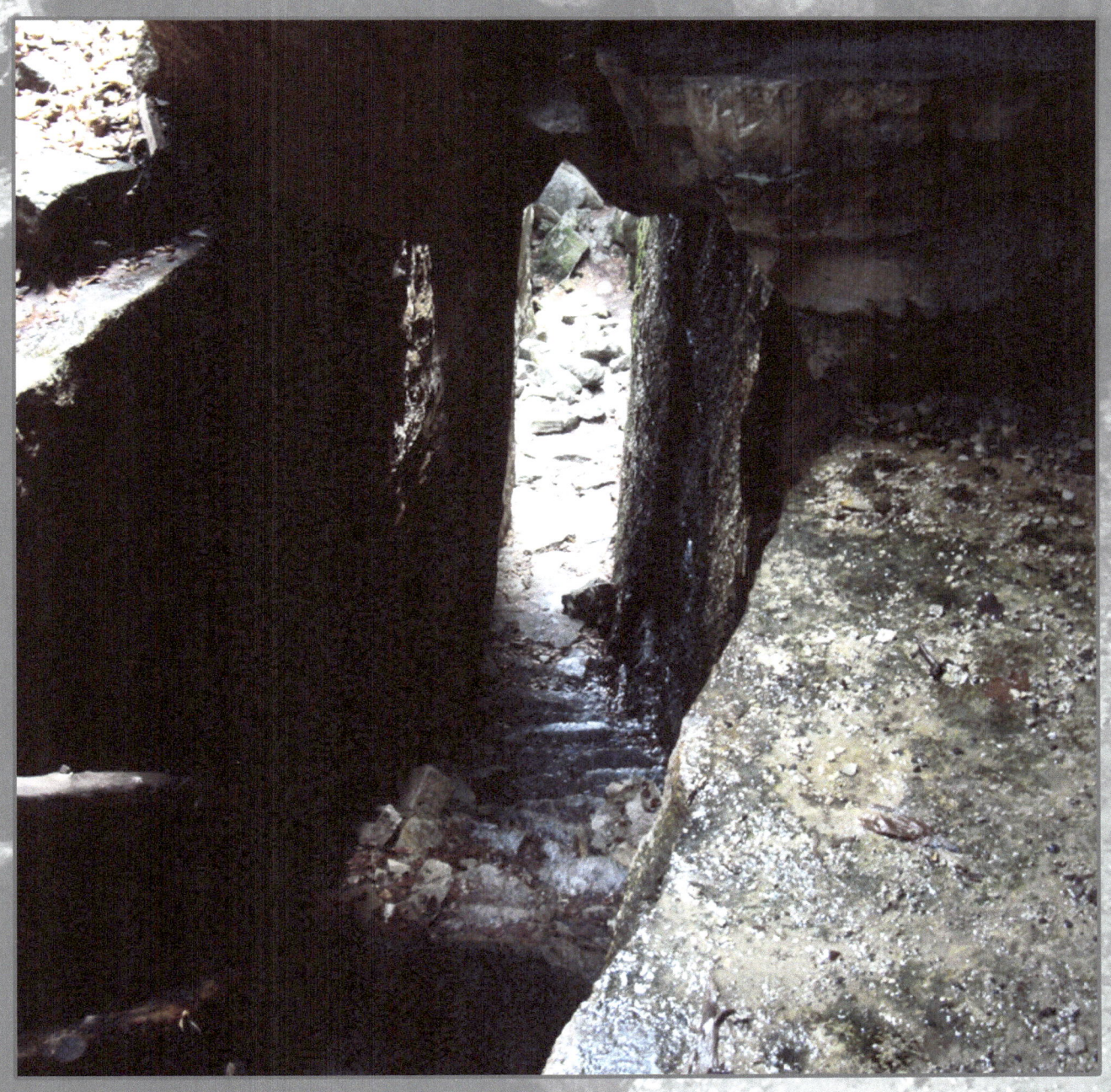

I am the door

And the doorman,

I am the lock

And the locksmith,

I am the guard

And the guarded.

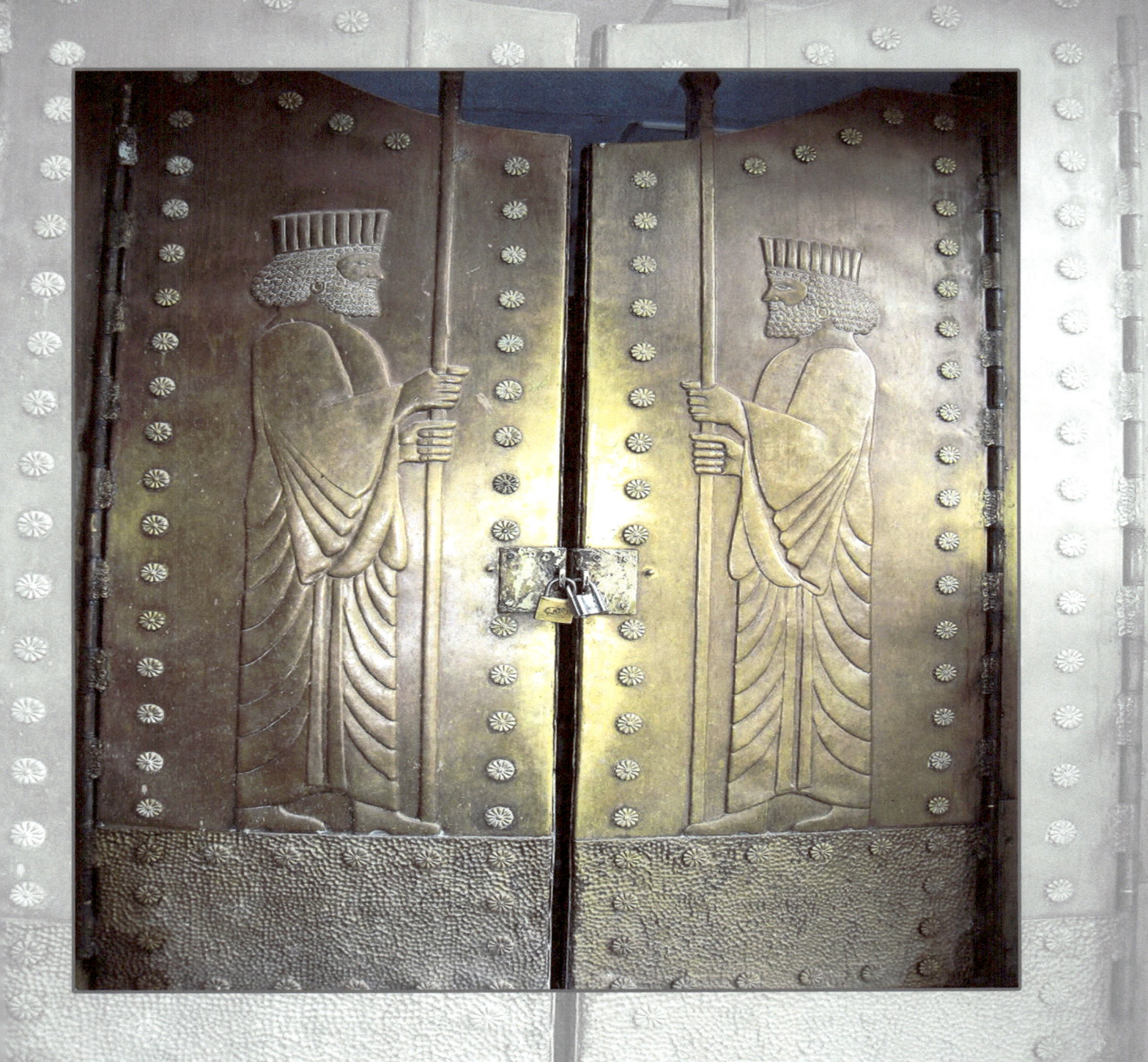

I am the door,

I am the one

　　　Transmitting

All the sounds

　　that come from

　　　the outer world.

You hear humming?

　　- It's a trumpet of spirit.

You hear drumming?

　　- It's your destiny's knock.

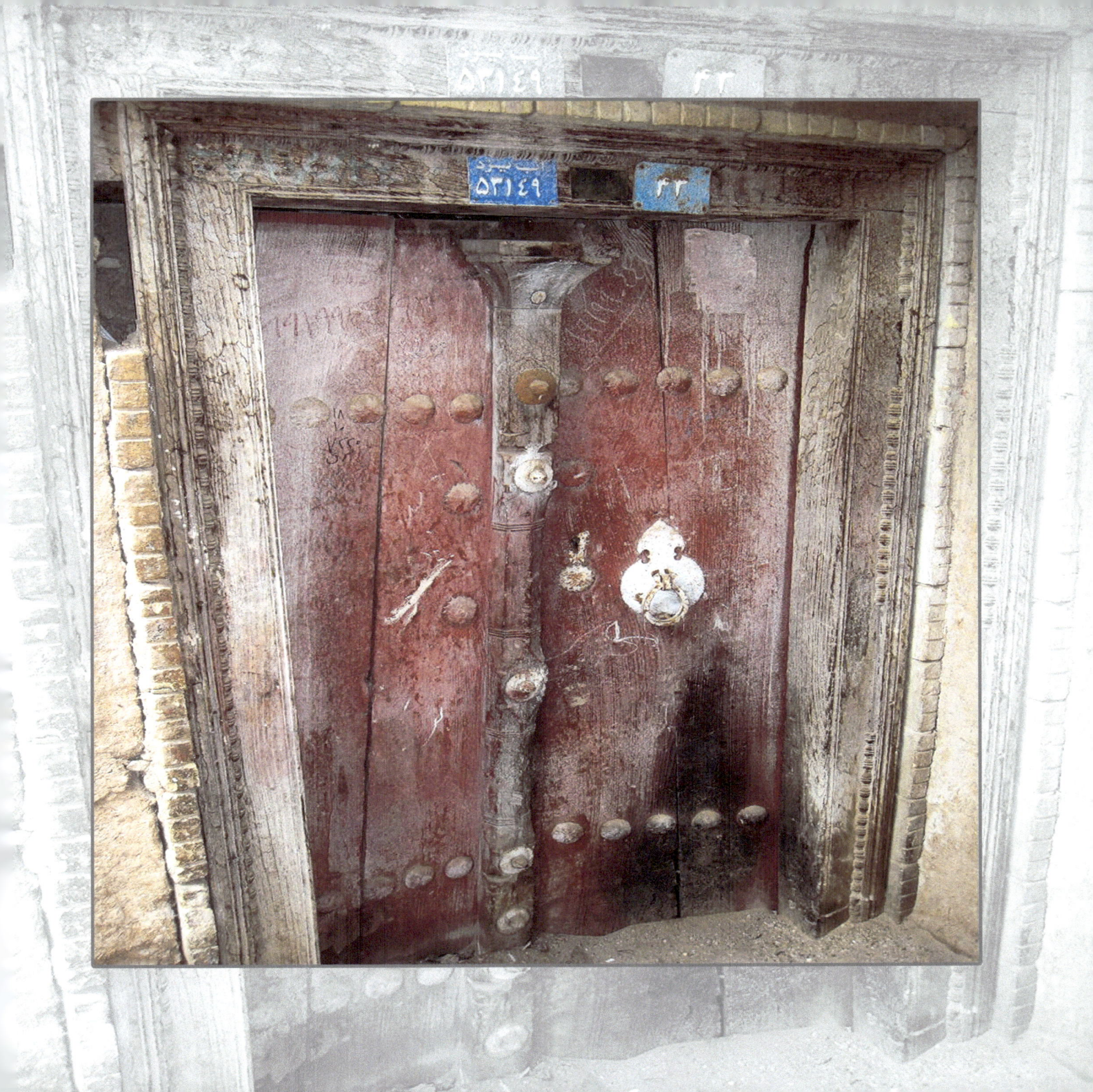

I am the door,
I am a channel
      connecting
      Past,
      Present,
      Future
And everything
      in between.
I link what soars above
To what lies beneath,
What's awake
      and what sleeps,
I am a switch.

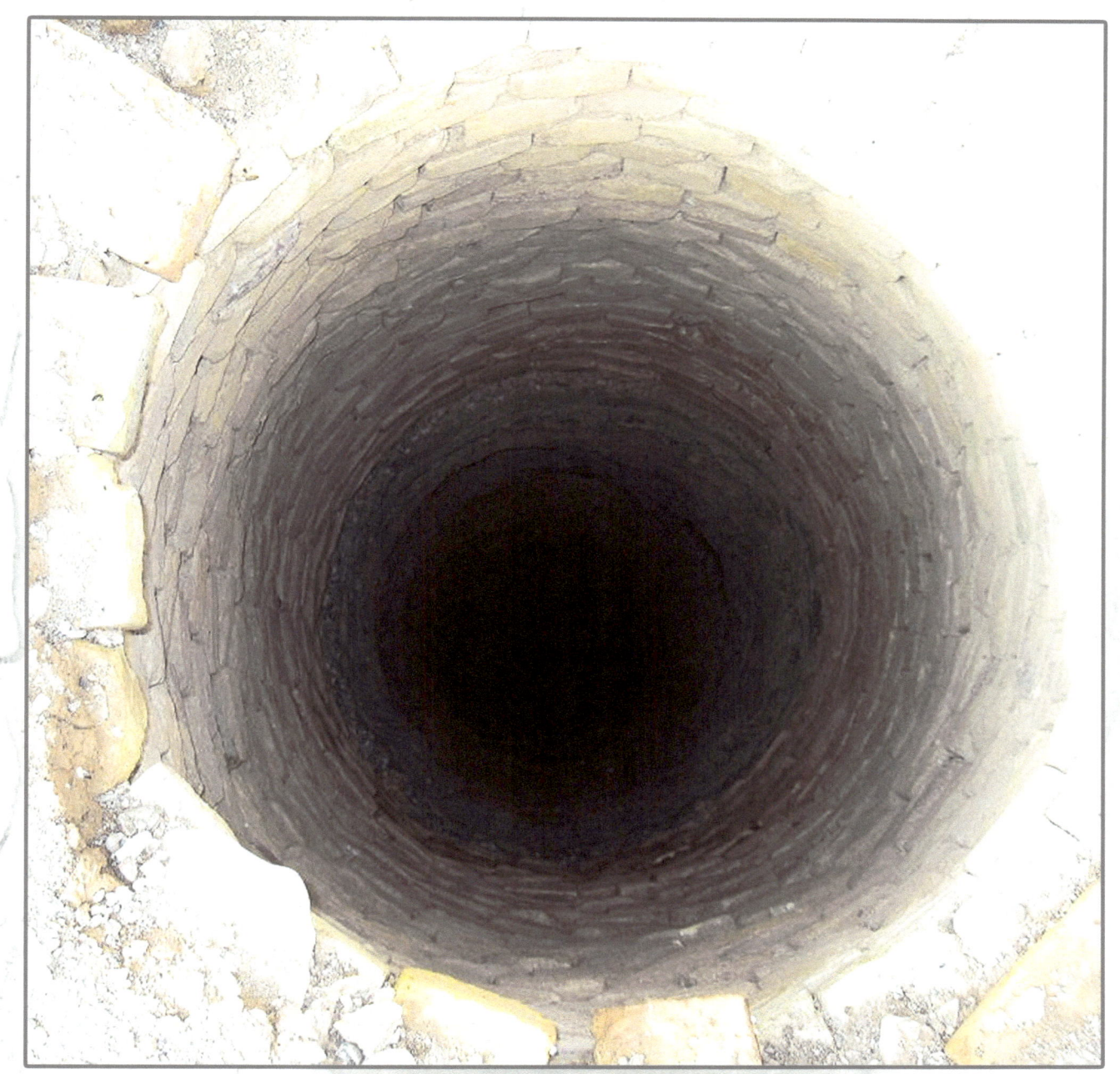

I am the door

Beyond the curtain

Of a waterfall

One must be clean

To be allowed

To witness what I guard

Let the water

Run through your flesh,

Let the rainbow

Pierce your heart

And enlighten your thoughts,

Maybe then

The curtain will open.

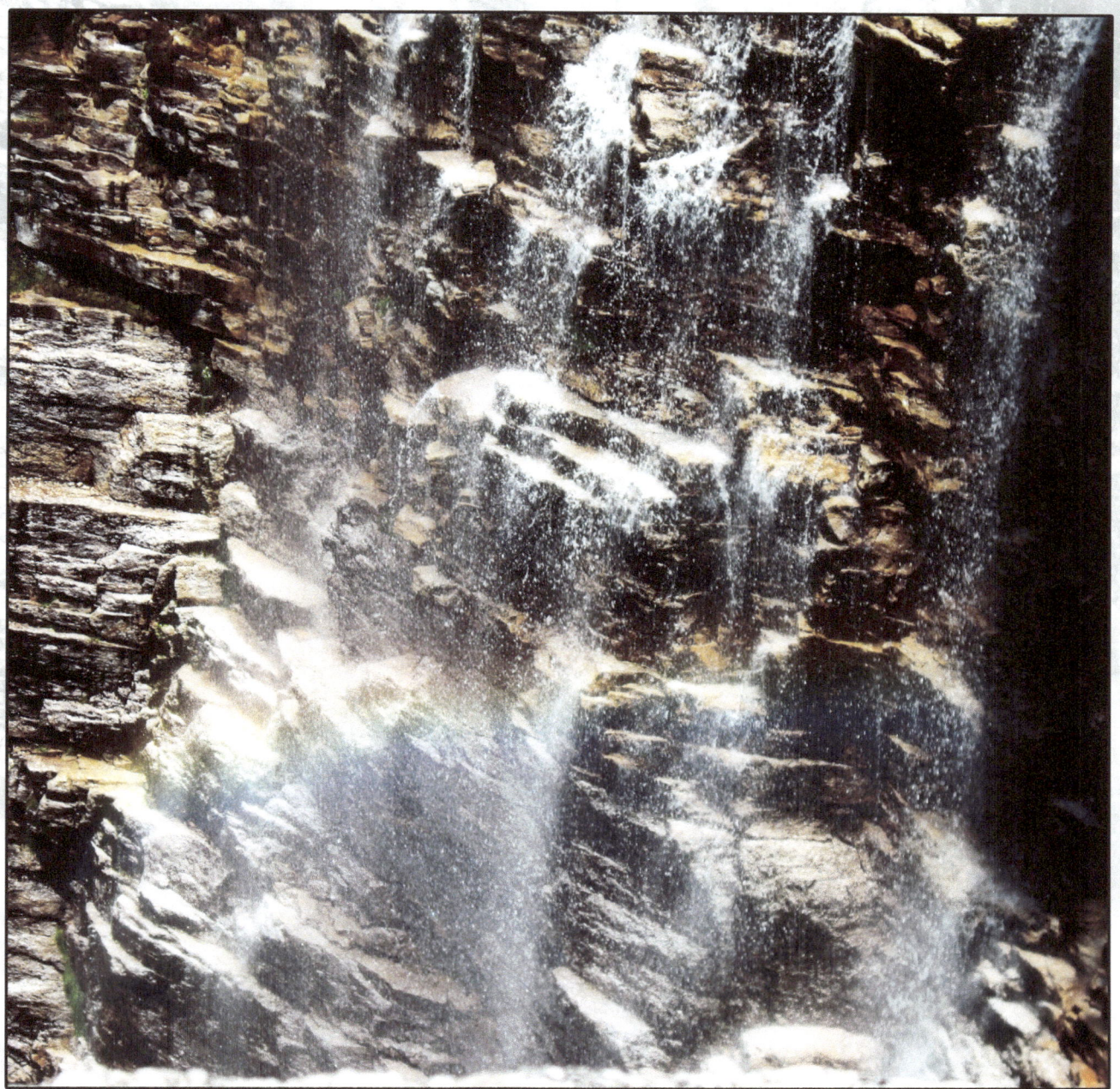

I am the door,

Let me be.

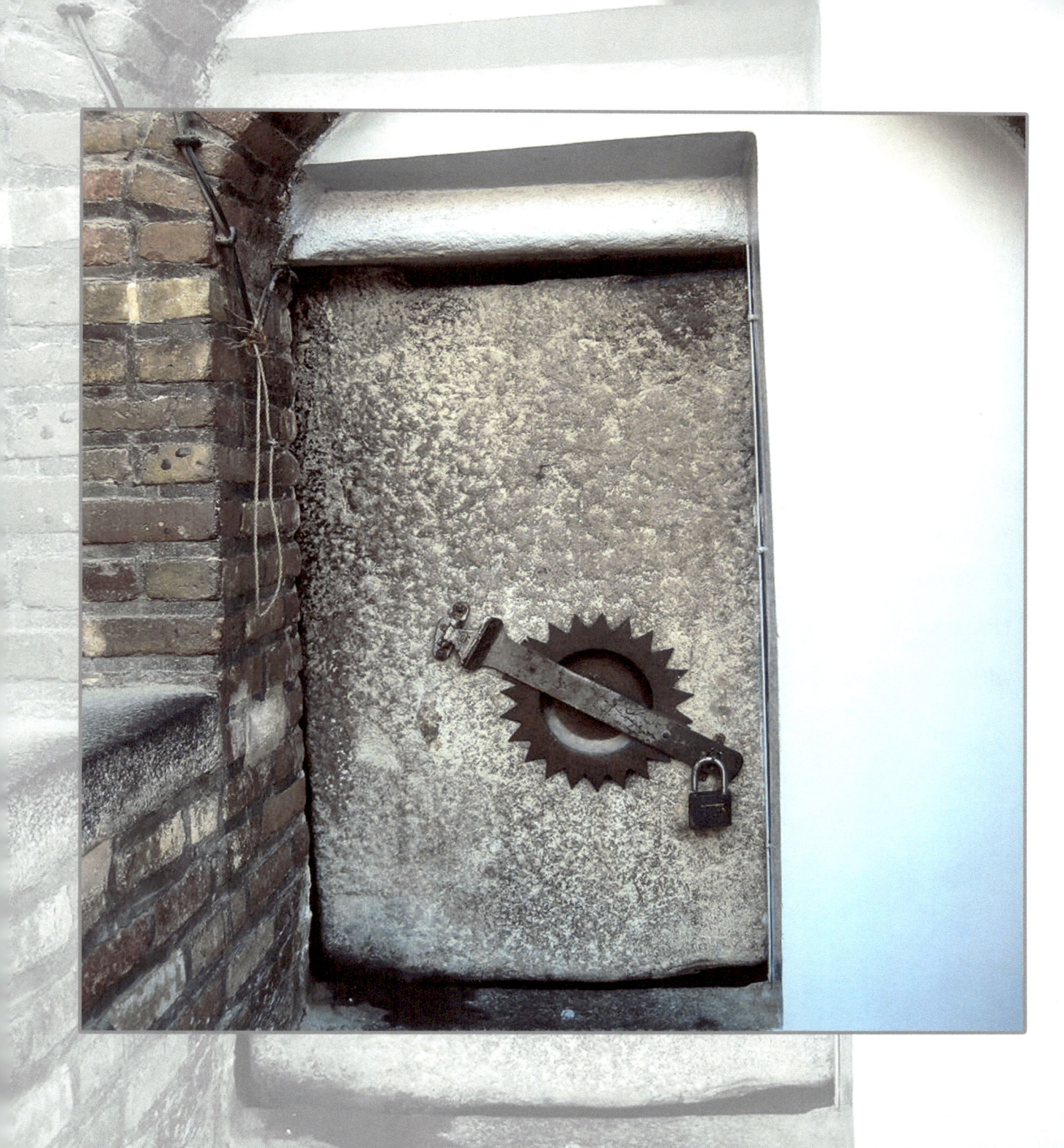

A **door** is a movable structure used to open and close off an entrance. When open, doors admit ventilation and light. The door is used to control the physical atmosphere within a space by enclosing the air drafts. Doors are significant in preventing the spread of fire. They also act as a barrier to noise. Doors also have an aesthetic role in creating an impression of what lies beyond. Doors are often symbolically endowed with ritual purposes, and the guarding or receiving of the keys to a door, or being granted access to a door can have special significance. Similarly, doors and doorways frequently appear in metaphorical or allegorical situations, literature and the arts, often as a portent of change.

Wikipedia

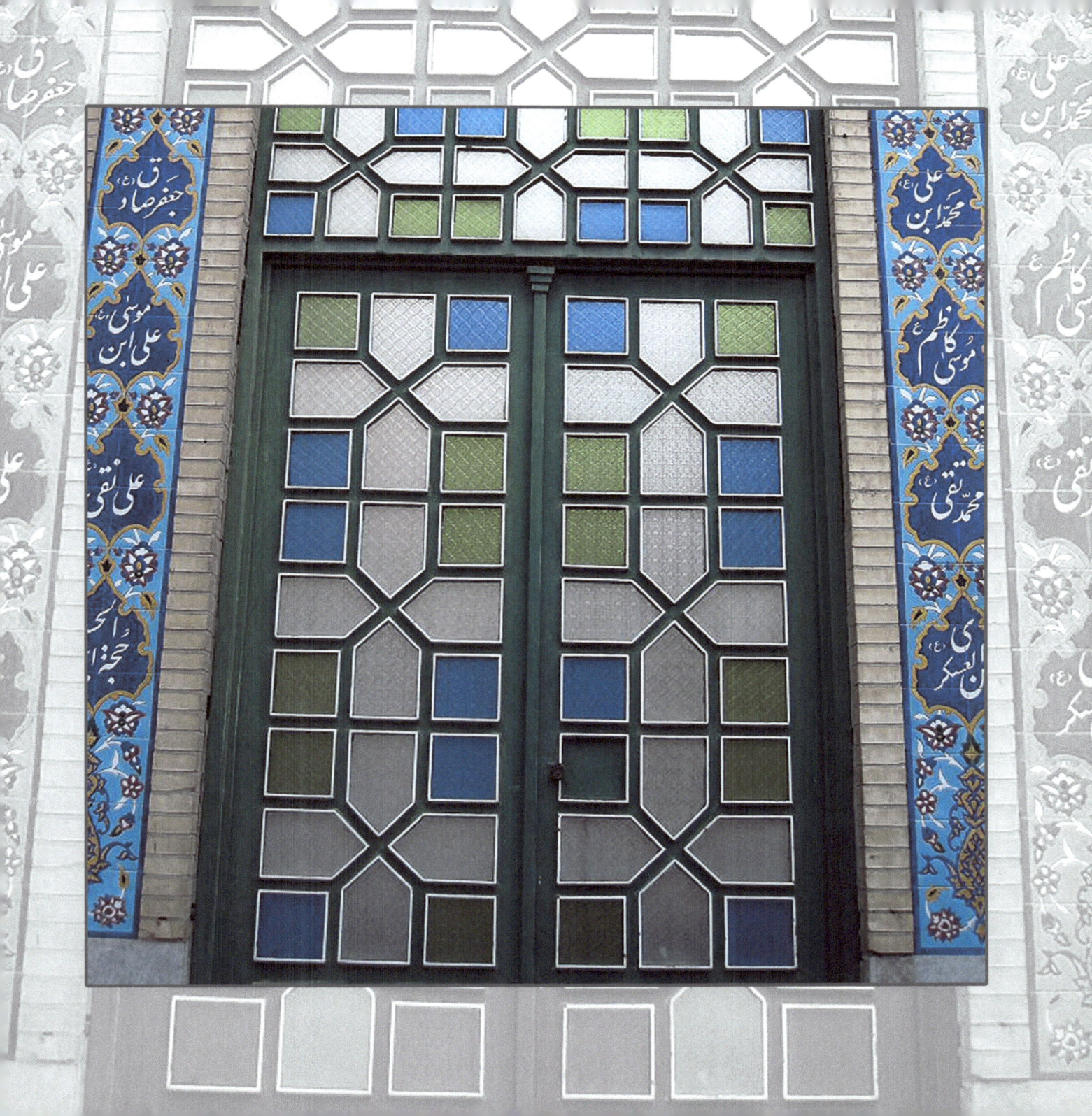

www.ingramcontent.com/pod-product-compliance
Lightning Source LLC
Chambersburg PA
CBHW051110180526
45172CB00002B/848